MW01515880

PALEO

CAST IRON
SKILLET
RECIPES

Louise Davidson

DISCLAIMER

All rights reserved. No part of this publication or the information in it may be quoted from or reproduced in any form by means such as printing, scanning, photocopying, or otherwise without prior written permission of the copyright holder.

Disclaimer and Terms of Use: Effort has been made to ensure that the information in this book is accurate and complete. However, the author and the publisher do not warrant the accuracy of the information, text, and graphics contained within the book due to the rapidly changing nature of science, research, known and unknown facts, and internet. The author and the publisher do not hold any responsibility for errors, omissions, or contrary interpretation of the subject matter herein. This book is presented solely for motivational and informational purposes only

TABLE OF CONTENTS

INTRODUCTION

To cook or not to cook – that is the question that comes across the minds of even the best of at-home chefs after a long and tiring day. Cooking can be a big production if you want to cook clean, healthy meals, and if you've switched over to the Paleo lifestyle, it can seem like an even greater challenge.

Paleo Cast Iron Recipes book is ready to rescue you from those mid-week cooking blues with simple recipes that can be whipped up in a single handy-dandy cast iron skillet. Yes, you read that right. Just one pan and you can have a meal that is fit for kings or for the royalty sitting at your very own table.

Cast iron cookware is great because of its versatility. It allows you to cook meals in one simple piece of cookware that would normally require all sorts of pots and pans. You can easily use cast iron on the stovetop for sautéing, stir-fry's, and soups, or use it in the oven, or both. Using cast iron for Paleo is particularly helpful since you can cook your proteins and veggies, from stovetop to oven, all in one dish.

Eating the Paleo way is an option many health-conscious families have embraced due to its focus on fresh, whole foods that are nutritious and free of dangerous additives that are used in processing. I won't go into the details of the Paleo diet since it is widely known and probably the main reason you got this book. If you want to familiarize yourself with the Paleo diet, I have added a few resources in the resources at the end of the book.

Today we have become used to easy-peasy meals in boxes, frozen dinners, and microwaveable feasts to help us out on those lazy days. However, if you've gone Paleo, that just isn't an option anymore, and that is why this book is here to help.

In this book, you will find a fantastic collection of recipes designed for the Paleo cook with precious time. The offerings include delicious meaty meals like Pancetta Meatballs and Beef Ragu or a Beef and Sweet Potato Casserole that is going to have everybody asking for seconds.

We've tried to give you some variety by taking this cookbook to all four corners of the globe, so be sure to try out Indian Chicken Biryani with Mint Chutney,

Cashew-Parm Chicken, or Fish Tacos with a lovely Orange Cilantro Salad.

The cookbook has a delicious selection of vegetarian dishes that you can use as sides or as a stand-alone meal. Plus, the sides section provides standard recipes like ZuCa Noodles and Flaxseed Tortillas to accompany other dishes.

With 35 recipes, you are guaranteed to have a month's worth of delicious Paleo meals that are easy to whip up in one dish. The dishes are clean, whole foods, and so delicious that you can bask in your at-home chef prowess without spending hours in the kitchen.

Let get busy in the kitchen!

Louise

YOUR CAST IRON SKILLET

Before we get into all the different recipes that you can use with the cast iron skillet, it is important to take the time to understand your cast iron skillet. Not using it properly can destroy your skillet quickly, but with proper care, cast iron can last for decades.

This chapter will cover everything you need to know about getting your cast iron skillet ready and keeping it perfect. If you have read any of my books Cooking with Cast Iron Skillets: Timeless and Delicious Family Recipes or Cooking with Cast Iron: More Timeless and Delicious Family Recipes, this chapter has the same information and you can skip it and go directly to the recipes.

The History of Cast Iron

While we often think of cast iron as something fairly new, it has actually been around since the 5th century BC. In fact, cast iron artefacts have been discovered from Ancient China, where it is believed to have been invented.

Originally used to make ploughshares, the Ancient Chinese also used it to make pots and even weapons. However, despite how old cast iron is, it did not come to Europe until the 15th century AD. During this time, cast iron was used for cannons.

In the 1700's, a man by the name of Abraham Darby began creating pots and kettles from cast iron when he found a way to produce the pots with a thinner amount of iron. It was through this process that owning cast iron became a popular choice, and cast iron cookware has been found in homes ever since.

Seasoning your Cast Iron

Although you may be able to purchase cast iron with a non-stick surface, the majority of cast iron skillets are not sold like that. Actually, I recommend getting an untreated cast iron skillet so that you can season it yourself.

While the term seasoning brings to mind adding spices, seasoning actually means making a cast iron skillet non-stick. This should be done before you cook on your cast iron skillet and any time your skillet begins to look dull.

To season your cast iron skillet, follow the steps below:

1. Preheat the oven to 350°F.

2. Wash the new skillet. This can be done with warm, soapy water, and a sponge. Do not use steel wool as you can scratch the pan and ruin it. Wash it thoroughly. It should be noted that this is the only time you use soapy water when cleaning the cast iron. After it is seasoned, do not use soap.

3. Rinse the skillet, and make sure that it is completely free of soap.

4. Dip a paper towel in vegetable oil.

5. Rub the oiled paper towel over the cast iron skillet. You should cover both the inside and outside of the cast iron skillet. Make sure it is a thick, even coat on the skillet.

6. Place in the preheated oven. Make sure the skillet is upside down and in the center of the oven. To catch oil drips, put a baking sheet or aluminum foil under it.

7. Bake the cast iron skillet for an hour. Do not remove it sooner than an hour or the seasoning process won't be perfect.

8. Turn off the oven, but leave the cast iron skillet in the oven.

9. Allow it to cool completely. Cast iron holds heat for a long time so it may take several hours to cool.

10. Wipe away any excess oil if necessary. You do not want to wipe all of the oil off. You want a smooth, shiny skillet but you don't want puddles of oil in your pan.

And that is all you need to do. Repeat whenever your skillet looks rusted or dull. General cooking, especially when using oil, will often keep the pan seasoned.

Maintenance for Your Cast Iron

Seasoning your cast iron skillet whenever it looks rusted or dull is the maintenance that you will do on a regular basis. Seasoning the skillet is very important and will help keep your skillet its best.

When it comes to washing your skillet, always rinse the skillet immediately after cooking. Run hot water over it, and wipe it clean. For food that is stuck on, use a non-metal brush and scrub with coarse salt. This will help remove the food without wrecking the skillet.

Dry the skillet thoroughly. Leaving a cast iron skillet wet will cause rust to form on the skillet, and this will shorten the life of your pan. If rust does form, use steel wool to remove the rust. Do not use it on other parts of the skillet. Once the rust is removed, go through the seasoning process with the skillet.

Finally, whenever you wash your skillet, spray it with a small amount cooking oil. Then place a paper towel inside the pan to store.

And that is all you need to do to maintain your cast iron skillet.

Health Benefits of Cast Iron

Although you wouldn't think of a skillet as something with health benefits, there are a number of health benefits that you can get by cooking with a cast iron skillet. These health benefits are:

1. You generally use less oil.

Because of how you season a cast iron skillet, you will find that your recipes do not require as much oil as they used to. This means less fat and food that has more flavor than grease. Both will help with your health. For one, you will enjoy the taste of your food and be less inclined to eat out and the other means that your meals are leaner.

2. You are exposed to fewer chemicals.

Cast iron is the natural choice when it comes to cooking. Most skillets that are not cast iron have a spray coating on them to make them non-stick. This coating contains several chemicals including perfluorocarbons, which are released into the air and into your food during cooking.

These chemicals are linked to liver damage, developmental problems in children and cancer.

Cast iron, as long has it has not been coated, is free from those chemicals and does not leave any chemicals in your food.

3. You will have an iron boost.

Finally, cast iron offers an increase of iron in your food, a huge benefit. Many people, especially women, have an iron deficiency. Cooking with cast iron helps boost iron by as much as 20% your daily iron intake.

Tips for Cooking with Cast Iron

The final thing that I want to touch on before we get into the recipes is to offer a few helpful tips that will make cooking with cast iron much easier. These are:

1. Always Preheat

Make sure that you always preheat your cast iron skillet. It can take a bit of time for the cast iron to heat up, so putting the food in too soon can cause your food to be undercooked or to take longer to cook. Preheating it will ensure that your food is being cooked on the best temperature every time.

2. Cook on Medium Temperatures

Although it does take time for cast iron to heat up, once it does, it maintains its heat for long periods. Cooking on high temperatures will result in your food burning, so always cook on medium temperatures -- medium-low through medium-high.

3. Don't Be Afraid to Make it Versatile

If there is a tool that is truly versatile it's the cast iron skillet. You can use it as a frying pan, a deep fryer, and even as a baking dish. One of the best things is that you can easily move your cast iron skillet from stove top to oven without having to do anything to it.

Experiment with your cast iron, and you will find it is really enjoyable to use. In fact, many of the recipes in this book will have you using your cast iron skillet as more than just a frying pan.

4. Reduce Cooking Times

Whenever you are using a recipe that is not designed for the cast iron skillet, make sure that you reduce cooking times a bit. Remember that the cast iron skillet maintains its heat for quite a while so you can cook the dish almost to completion, turn down the temperature or turn off the stove, and let the pan do the rest of the cooking.

Note: Always watch your food if you are leaving it in the cast iron skillet for serving since the food can burn if the pan is still hot.

5. Watch that Heat

Finally, watch the temperature of the pan. Since the handles are not covered, they will get as hot as the pan itself. It's a good idea to always wear oven mitts when handling your cast iron skillet to prevent burns.

So now that you know the tips; grab your cast iron skillets and let's get started on the recipes!

CHICKEN

Chicken Biryani with Mint Chutney

Serves: 4
Preparation time: 20 minutes
Cooking time: 25 minutes

Ingredients:
4 x 4 oz chicken breasts
1 medium carrot, peeled, grated
½ head cauliflower, stemmed
1 small onion, diced
¼ cup cashews, halved
½ cup almonds, chopped
1 tsp curry powder
½ tsp cumin seeds
2 cups low-sodium organic chicken stock
1 tsp salt, black pepper
Coconut oil

Mint Chutney
2 cups mint, stemmed
2 dates, pitted
¼ cup coconut oil
½ cup balsamic vinegar
½ tsp salt
½ tsp black pepper

Directions:
1. Place cauliflower in food processor, and pulse until you have small, rice-like granules, then set aside.
2. Slice chicken breast into 1" pieces.

3. Heat 4 tbsp. coconut oil in cast iron skillet
4. Add chicken breast, brown, then remove from skillet onto dish.
5. Pour another tbsp. of oil into skillet, add cumin, and toast for a 15 seconds, then add onions, carrots, cashews, and almonds, and sauté.
6. Return chicken to skillet, add curry powder, black pepper, salt, and chicken stock. Cover skillet and bring to a boil.
7. Reduce heat to medium-low, and cook for 15 minutes or until cauliflower is tender.
8. While biryani is cooking, combine ingredients for chutney in blender, mix until well-combined.
9. Serve biryani with a dollop of mint chutney and a green side salad.

Nutrition (per serving)
Calories 577 g
Carbs 18 g
Fat 39 g
Protein 39 g
Sodium 1078 mg
Sugar 6 g

Serves: 6
Preparation time: 10 minutes
Cooking time: 30 minutes

Ingredients:
1 lb chicken breast
½ lb Polish sausage
1 green bell pepper, seeded, diced
1 carrot, peeled, diced
1 celery stalk, diced
1 red onion, sliced
1 head cauliflower
2 cups tomatoes, diced
2 cups low-sodium chicken stock
1 tsp oregano, paprika, cayenne pepper
1 tsp black pepper
1 tsp salt
1 bay leaf
Extra virgin olive oil

Directions:
1. Chop chicken breast and Polish sausage into ½" pieces.
2. Grate cauliflower.
3. Heat 3 tbsp. extra virgin olive oil in cast iron skillet over medium heat.
4. Sauté chicken and Polish sausage for five minutes.
5. Add onion and garlic and sauté for a minute.
6. Add bell pepper, celery stalk, and carrot, and sauté for 3 minutes.

7. Add tomatoes, chicken stock, black pepper, cauliflower and spices.
8. Cover skillet and cook for 20 minutes over medium heat.
9. Serve hot.

Nutrition (per serving)
Calories 503 g
Carbs 14 g
Fat 28 g
Protein 51 g
Sodium 1245 mg
Sugar 7 g

Serves: 4
Preparation time: 15 minutes
Cooking time: 1hour

Ingredients:
8 chicken thighs, skinless
1 cup artichoke hearts
8 shitake mushrooms, sliced
1 red onion, sliced
2 cloves garlic
1 carrot, diced
2 tbsp fresh dill
1 tsp salt
1 tsp black pepper
Coconut oil

Directions:
1. Preheat oven to 375ºF.
2. Heat 4 tbsp. coconut oil in skillet, add chicken thighs, brown, and remove thighs to plate.
3. Into same skillet, add garlic and onion, and sauté for a minute.
4. Stir in shitake mushrooms, artichoke hearts, carrot, dill, salt and black pepper.
5. Place chicken thighs on vegetables, cover skillet with lid or aluminium foil, and bake in oven for 40 minutes.

Nutrition (per serving)

Calories 711 g

Carbs 30 g

Fat 28 g

Protein 85 g

Sodium 1221 mg

Sugar 8 g

Cashew-Parm Chicken

Serves: 5-6
Preparation time: Overnight +15 min.
Cooking time: 40

Ingredients:

4 x 4 oz chicken breasts, skinless, boneless
1 cup organic tomato sauce
¾ cup cashews
4 cloves garlic, minced
1 large onion, diced
1 tsp oregano
1 bay leaf
1 lemon, juiced
Salt, black pepper
Coconut oil

Directions:

1. Crush cashews in a food processor. Add lemon juice, and leave overnight.
2. Preheat oven to 375°F.
3. Heat 4 tbsp. extra virgin olive oil in cast iron skillet over medium heat.
4. Place chicken breasts in skillet, brown, remove to plate.
5. Add garlic and onions to pan, and sauté for approximately 30 seconds.
6. Add tomato sauce, chicken stock, oregano, bay leaf, salt and black pepper, and bring to boil.
7. Return chicken breast to pan, sprinkle with cashew cheese, cover with lid or aluminium paper, and bake in oven for 30 minutes.
8. Remove bay leaf before serving.

Nutrition (per serving)

Calories 676 g

Carbs 32 g

Fat 49 g

Protein 34 g

Sodium 426 mg

Sugar 12 g

Chicken with Spinach and Raspberry Stuffing

Serves: 4
Preparation time: 25 minutes
Cooking time: 25 minutes

Ingredients:
4 x 4 oz chicken breasts
4 slices bacon
4 cups fresh spinach, chopped
½ cup frozen or fresh raspberries
½ cup cashews, chopped
Salt, black pepper
Coconut oil

Directions:
1. Preheat oven to 400°F.
2. Create a slit in the side of each chicken breast, and slice in half about three-quarters of the way through.
3. Combine spinach, cashews, and a tsp salt and black pepper, along with 3 tbsp. coconut oil. Blend until combined but chunky.
4. Using a spoon, mix raspberries into the spinach mixture.
5. Spoon spinach into the slit part of chicken breast, wrap each breast in a slice of bacon.
6. Heat 4 tbsp. coconut oil in cast iron skillet, carefully place each breast in skillet, and brown both sides.
7. Place cast iron skillet into oven, and bake for 20 minutes.
8. Serve with Toasted Pecan and Cranberry Salad (recipe in Sides and Accompaniments).

Nutrition (per serving)
Calories 606 g
Carbs 24 g
Fat 45 g
Protein 32 g
Sodium 87 mg
Sugar 8 g

Serves: 6
Preparation time: 10 minutes
Cooking time: 45 minutes

Ingredients:
1 lb chicken breasts, skinless, boneless
½ lb shiitake mushrooms
4 cups low-sodium chicken stock
2 tbsp ginger, grated
2 tsp lemongrass, minced
2 carrots, diced
1 onion, peeled, sliced
4 cloves garlic, minced
½ tsp salt
1 tsp black pepper
1 tbsp coconut aminos
Extra light olive oil

Directions:
1. Slice chicken breasts into ½" pieces.
2. Heat 4 tablespoons olive oil in cast iron pot over medium heat, add chicken, brown, and remove chicken breast to plate.
3. Add onions and garlic to same pot, sauté for 30 seconds, add ginger, mushrooms, carrots, lemongrass, and sauté for two minutes.
4. Stir in chicken stock, salt, black pepper, and coconut aminos, cover and simmer for 35 minutes on medium low.

Nutrition per serving

Calories 278 g

Carbs 17 g

Fat 2 g

Sodium 654 mg

Protein 28 g

Sugar 5 g

Chicken with Asparagus Bacon Bundles

Serves: 4
Preparation time: 10 minutes
Cooking time: 45 minutes

Ingredients:
4 x 4 oz chicken breasts
12 asparagus spears, trimmed
4 slices bacon
½ cup water
Salt, black pepper
½ tsp paprika
¼ cup ghee
Extra virgin olive oil

Directions:
1. Preheat oven to 375°F.
2. Wrap each asparagus stalk with one slice of bacon.
3. Heat ghee in cast iron skillet over medium heat, add paprika.
4. Into ghee, place chicken breasts. Brown.
5. Place asparagus bacon bundles into skillet alongside chicken.
6. Place skillet into oven, and bake for 35 minutes.

Nutrition (per serving)
Calories 360
Carbs 3 g
Fat 26 g
Protein 29 g
Sodium 214 mg
Sugar 1 g

Serves: 4
Preparation time: 15 minutes.
Cooking time: 35 minutes

Ingredients:
1 lb chicken breast
1 cup tomato puree
3 dates, pitted
½ cup cashew, chopped
1 lemon, juiced
1 clove garlic, minced
1 tsp oregano
1 tsp salt
1 tsp black pepper
Extra virgin olive oil

Directions:
1. Preheat oven to 375ºF.
2. Place dates in food processor and mix into paste. Add garlic, lemon juice and tomato puree, mix, set aside.
3. Using mallet, pound chicken breasts until they are ¼" thick (or ask your butcher to do it).
4. Heat tbsp. extra virgin olive oil in skillet over medium heat, place chicken breasts in skillet so that they completely cover bottom of pan, turn over after 30 seconds.
5. Pour blender sauce over chicken, top with cashews, and slide into oven for 30 minutes.
6. Slice and serve.

Nutrition (per serving)

Calories 345 g

Carbs 17g

Fat 19 g

Sodium 643 mg

Protein 29 g

Sugar 8 g

BEEF

Red Beef Curry

Serves: 4-6
Preparation time: 10 minutes
Cooking time: 30 minutes

Ingredients:
16 oz sirloin steak
1 red bell pepper, seeded, diced
1 medium carrot, peeled, grated
1 medium onion, diced
¼ cup cashews, halved
1 tbsp tomato paste
½ tsp turmeric
¼ tsp cinnamon
1 tsp curry powder
2 cups low-sodium organic chicken stock
1 cup coconut milk
1 tsp salt, black pepper
Coconut oil

Directions:
1. Slice steak against the grain into ½" wide strips.
2. Heat 4 tbsp. coconut oil in cast iron skillet over medium-high heat, add steak and sauté for two minutes, remove from pan.
3. Add a little more coconut oil to pan if necessary, add onion, garlic, and give a quick sauté until garlic is fragrant.
4. Add carrot, bell pepper, and cashews, and sauté for another minute.

5. Mix in tomato paste, turmeric, cinnamon, curry powder.
6. Add in coconut milk, chicken stock, salt, and black pepper, and cover skillet and bring to simmer.
7. Reduce heat to low. and cook for 20 minutes.
8. Serve Red Beef Curry with Cauliflower Rice.

Nutrition (per serving)
Calories 630 g
Carbs 23 g
Fat 47 g
Sodium 619 mg
Protein 33 g
Sugar 10 g

Pancetta Meatballs with Red Bell Slaw

Serves: 24 meatballs
Preparation time: 15 minutes
Cooking time: 25 minutes

Ingredients:
1 lb lean ground beef
½ lb Pancetta, chopped
1 small onion, minced
4 cloves garlic, minced
1 large onion, sliced
1 tbsp coconut flour
1 egg
3 red bell peppers, seeded, julienned
1 lemon, juiced
½ tsp oregano
Salt and pepper
Extra light olive oil

Directions:
1. Preheat oven to 400ºF.
2. Crack egg into large bowl and whisk.
3. Add ground beef, pancetta, minced onion, garlic, coconut flour, oregano, 1 tsp salt, and 1 tsp black pepper, and combine.
4. Roll into 1" meatballs.
5. Heat 4 tbsp. extra virgin olive oil in cast iron skillet.
6. Place meatballs in skillet, brown, and slide skillet into oven for 15 minutes.
7. Combine bell peppers, onions with 5 tbsp. extra virgin olive oil, lemon, salt, black pepper to taste.
8. Serve meatballs with bell pepper and onion slaw.

Nutrition (per serving)

Calories 110 g

Carbs 3 g

Fat 7 g

Sodium 235 mg

Protein 10 g

Sugar 1 g

Beef Ragu

Serves: 4
Preparation time: 20 minutes
Cooking time: 30 minutes

Ingredients:
1 lb stewing beef, cubed
1 celery stalk, diced
1 onion, diced
2 carrots, diced
1 cup tomatoes, diced
8 cloves garlic, minced
2 cups chicken stock
1 tsp rosemary
1 tsp salt
1 tsp black pepper
Extra virgin olive oil

Directions
1. Preheat oven to 350ºF.
2. Heat 5 tbsp. extra virgin olive oil in cast iron skillet over medium-high heat.
3. Add beef and brown.
4. Reduce heat to medium-low add onion and garlic, and sauté for a minute.
5. Stir in carrots, celery, rosemary, salt, and black pepper, and cook for 5 minutes.
6. Add chicken stock and tomato, and cover.
7. Place cast iron skillet in oven, and cook for 2 hours.
8. Serve Beef Ragu over ZuCa Noodles (recipe in Sides and Accompaniments).

Nutrition (per serving)

Calories 319 g

Carbs 10 g

Fat 15 g

Protein 36 g

Sodium 1067 mg

Sugar 4 g

Beef and Sweet Potato Casserole

Serves: 5-6
Preparation time: 15 minutes
Cooking time: 45 minutes

Ingredients:
1 lb ground beef
3 sweet potatoes
1 medium onion, sliced
½ cup cashews
1 cup coconut milk
½ tsp thyme
Salt and black pepper
Extra virgin olive oil

Directions:
1. Preheat oven to 375ºF.
2. Peel sweet potatoes and slice into ½" rounds.
3. Place 4 tbsp. extra virgin olive oil in skillet, and heat over medium-high heat.
4. Add onion and garlic, and sauté for 30 seconds.
5. Add beef and brown. Stir in 1 tsp salt and thyme, remove from heat.
6. Top beef with sweet potato slices, sprinkle with ½ tsp salt, black pepper.
7. Cover potatoes with coconut milk and sprinkle cashews. Cover with lid or aluminum foil.
8. Bake casserole in oven for 40 minutes.
9. Cool for 10 minutes before serving.

Nutrition (per serving)
Calories 493 g
Carbs 43 g
Fat 25 g
Protein 28 g
Sodium 70 mg
Sugar 3 g

Steak and Broccoli Soup

Serves: 4
Preparation time: 15 minutes
Cooking time: 45 minutes

Ingredients:
1 lb sirloin steak
5 cups broccoli florets
4 cloves garlic, minced
1 medium onion, diced
1 tsp coconut flour
1 lemon, juiced
1 tsp red pepper flakes
1 tsp salt
1 tsp black pepper
¼ cup ghee, melted
4 cups low-sodium beef stock
Coconut oil

Directions:
1. Combine ghee with coconut flour, set aside.
2. Heat 4 tbsp. coconut oil in cast iron pot, add steak and sauté for two minutes.
3. Remove steak from pot.
4. Into same pot, add garlic and onion, sauté for 30 seconds.
5. Add broccoli, continue to sauté for another minute.
6. Return steak to pot, add chicken stock, lemon juice, red pepper, salt, and black pepper. Cover pot, bring to boil, reduce heat to low.
7. Pour 3 tbsp. of liquid from pot, and mix into ghee, add ghee mixture to the pot, and simmer on low for 35 minutes.

Nutrition per serving
Calories 481
Carbs 12 g
Fat 31 g
Sodium 837 mg
Protein 40 g
Sugar 3 g

Succulent Steak Salad with Sweet Potato

Serves: 6
Preparation time: 15 minutes
Cooking time: 30 minutes

Ingredients:
2 x 8 oz top sirloin steak
12 cherry tomatoes, halved
1 English cucumber, sliced
2 cups arugula, chopped
1 cup green lettuce, chopped
1 large sweet potato
1 tsp salt
1 tsp black pepper
Extra light olive oil

Directions:
1. Slice sweet potatoes into ½"-thick rounds.
2. Heat 3 tbsp. extra virgin olive oil in cast iron skillet.
3. Cook sweet potatoes approximately 8 minutes per side or until tender, and remove to plate.
4. Into same cast iron skillet place top sirloin steaks, cook 5-6 minutes per side for medium-rare, remove to plate.
5. In a large bowl combine arugula, lettuce, cucumbers, tomato.
6. Evenly divide salad among four plates. Place a few potato discs per plate.
7. Slice top sirloin against the grain into ¼" slices and place atop the salad.
8. Top with Paleo Ranch Dressing (recipe in Sides and Condiments) and serve.

Nutrition per serving:

Calories 395 g

Carbs 27 g

Fat 15 g

Sodium 700 mg

Protein 40 g

Sugar 14 g

Mini Eggplant Lasagna

Serves: 4
Preparation time: 10 minutes
Cooking time: 50 minutes

Ingredients:
1 lb lean ground beef
4 Chinese eggplants
1 medium onion, diced
4 cloves garlic
2 cups tomato puree
1 lemon, juiced
1 tsp black pepper
1 tsp salt
Extra light olive oil

Directions:
1. Preheat oven to 400°F.
2. Slice eggplant in half horizontally and in half again vertically.
3. Heat 4 tbsp. extra virgin olive oil in cast iron skillet.
4. Add ground beef, brown, remove to plate.
5. Add garlic, onion, sauté.
6. Pour tomato puree into skillet, mix.
7. Set eggplant in skillet flesh-side up.
8. Spoon beef onto flesh of each eggplant, ladle some of the tomato puree on top of eggplant.
9. Cover skillet and bake in oven for 40 minutes.

Nutrition (per serving)

Calories 476 g

Carbs 49 g

Fat 15 g

Protein 43 g

Sodium 704 mg

Sugar 24 g

PORK AND LAMB

Pork and Broccoli Skillet

Serves: 4
Preparation time: 10 minutes
Cooking time: 20 minutes

Ingredients:
1 lb pork loin roast
4 cups broccoli florets
4 cloves garlic, minced
1 medium onion, diced
¼ cup coconut aminos
½ tsp salt
1 tsp black pepper
1 cup low-sodium beef stock
Coconut oil

Directions:
1. Slice pork loin roast into 1" pieces.
2. Heat 4 tbsp. coconut oil into cast iron skillet, add pork and sauté for two minutes.
3. Remove pork from skillet.
4. Into same pot, add garlic and onion, sauté for 30 seconds.
5. Add broccoli, continue to sauté for another minute.
6. Return pork to pot, add beef stock, coconut aminos, salt, black pepper, cover and cook on low for 15 mins.

Nutrition (per serving)

Calories 376 g

Carbs 10 g

Fat 22 g

Sodium 430 mg

Protein 36 g

Sugar 3 g

BBQ Pork chops

Serves: 6
Preparation time: 20 minutes
Cooking time: 45 minutes

Ingredients:

4 x 4 oz boneless pork chops
2 cups tomato puree
3 dates, pitted
½ cup cashew, chopped
1 lemon, juiced
1 clove garlic, minced
1 tsp oregano
1 tsp salt
1 tsp black pepper
Extra light olive oil

Directions:

1. Preheat oven to 400°F.
2. Place dates in food processor and mix into paste. Add garlic, lemon juice, and tomato puree, mix, set aside.
3. Heat 4 tbsp. extra virgin olive oil in cast iron skillet over medium-high heat.
4. Sear pork chops, top with BBQ sauce from blender, slide into oven, and cook for 35 minutes, turning halfway through.
5. Serve with Garlic Asparagus Sauté (recipe in Vegetarian).

Nutrition (per serving):
Calories 487 g
Carbs 24 g
Fat 35 g
Protein 23 g
Sodium 676 mg
Sugar 11 g

Pork Loin with Sweet Potato

Serves: 2
Preparation time: 15 minutes
Cooking time: 55 minutes

Ingredients:
1 lb pork loin roast
1 sweet potato, peeled, sliced
1 red apple, cored, sliced
1 celery stalk, chopped
1 clove garlic, minced
1 tsp salt
1 tsp black pepper
Extra virgin olive oil

Directions:
1. Preheat oven to 400ºF.
2. Heat 4 tbsp. extra virgin olive oil in skillet, place pork loin in skillet and brown.
3. Remove pork loin to plate.
4. Place sweet potato, apples, onions, celery, garlic on bottom of cast iron skillet, top with pork loin roast, and slide into oven for 45 minutes.

Nutrition per serving:
Calories 375 g
Carbs 19 g
Fat 18 g
Sodium 672 mg
Protein 34 g
Sugar 9 g

Lamb and Butternut Squash Stew

Serves: 4
Preparation time: 15 minutes
Cooking time: 50 minutes

Ingredients:
1 butternut squash
12 oz lamb
1 medium onion, sliced
3 cups water
3 tbsp ghee
½ lemon, juiced
Salt and black pepper

Garnish
Parsley

Directions:
1. Peel butternut squash, chop into 1" cubes, place aside.
2. Cut lamb into 1" cubes.
3. Heat ghee in cast iron pot, add lamb and brown.
4. Add onion, sauté.
5. Add butternut squash, lemon juice, water and salt, black pepper to taste.
6. Cover cast iron pot, and cook for 45 minutes or until squash is tender.

Nutrition (per serving)

Calories 361 g

Carbs 15 g

Fat 23 g

Protein 25 g

Sodium 75 mg

Sugar 4

Middle Eastern Spiced Lamb

Serve: 6
Preparation time: 5 minutes
Cooking time: 50 minutes

Ingredients:
2 lb boneless lamb loin
¼ cup dried apricots
¼ cup walnuts
¼ cup plum
3 tsp ginger, grated
1 tsp cinnamon
1 tsp salt
1 tsp black pepper
Coconut oil

Directions:
1. Preheat oven to 400ºF.
2. Slice boneless lamb chops into1" cubes and sprinkle with 1 tsp salt.
3. Heat 4 tbsp. coconut oil in cast iron skillet over medium heat.
4. Brown lamb.
5. Reduce heat to medium low, add apricots, walnuts, plum ginger cinnamon, salt, black pepper.
6. Place into oven for 45 minutes.
7. Serve with Flax Tortilla (recipe in Sides and Accompaniments) for scooping.

Nutrition per serving (g)

Calories 400 g

Fat 22 g

Carbs 6 g

Protein 42 g

Sodium 488 mg

Sugar 4 g

FISH

Wild Salmon with Yellow Squash

Serves: 4
Preparation time: 15 minutes
Cooking time: 15 minutes

Ingredients:
4 x 4 oz wild salmon fillets (1" thick)
2 medium yellow squash, sliced
2 fennel bulbs, sliced into strips
¼ cup sliced almonds
1 lemon, juiced
1 tsp lemon peel, grated
¼ cup ghee
Salt and black pepper
Almond oil

Directions:
1. Heat almond oil in your cast iron skillet over medium heat.
2. Add squash, fennel, and almonds, and sauté until veggies are tender. Remove to dish and toss with lemon juice, salt, and black pepper.
3. Add ghee into same cast iron skillet, and heat on medium.
4. Place salmon fillets skin-side up in heated skillet. Cook for 5 minutes, gently turn over, and cook for 4 minutes.
5. Serve salmon with veggies.

Nutrition (per serving)

Calories 451 g
Carbs 13 g
Fat 32 g
Protein 28 g
Sodium 124 mg
Sugar 2 g

Prosciutto-Wrapped Cod Filet and Zucchini

Serves: 4
Preparation time: 10 minutes
Cooking time: 20 minutes

Ingredients:

4 x 4 oz cod filets
4 slices prosciutto ham
2 cups chicken stock
¼ cup sundried tomato, chopped
2 cloves garlic, grated
Salt and black pepper
Coconut oil

Directions:

1. Preheat oven to 400ºF.
2. In bowl combine garlic, ½ tsp salt, ½ tsp black pepper and mix.
3. Wrap each cod fillet with a prosciutto slice.
4. Heat 4 tbsp. coconut oil in cast iron skillet, add cod filets to skillet and cook 3 minutes per side.
5. Add sundried tomato and garlic mixture to skillet, and place into the oven for 15 minutes.
6. Plate prosciutto-wrapped cod fillet with ZuCa Noodles (recipe in Sides and Accompaniments).

Nutrition (per serving)

Calories 504 g

Carbs 35 g

Fat 28 g

Protein 34 g

Sodium 1807 mg

Sugar 13 g

Serves: 4
Preparation time: 10 minutes
Cooking time: 10 minutes

Ingredients
16 oz Tilapia filets
1 tsp fresh ginger, grated
½ red bell pepper, seeded, diced
1 green onion, chopped
1 green chili pepper, seeded, minced
8 leaves Boston lettuce
2 cups cilantro, chopped
1/3 cup natural orange juice
1 tbsp coconut aminos
Extra virgin olive oil
Salt and black pepper

Directions:
1. For the filling, heat 4 tbsp. of extra virgin olive oil in cast iron skillet on medium heat. Place Tilapia filets in cast iron skillet, and cook for 4 minutes per side.
2. Remove fish to plate, and using fork, separate fish into small pieces. Mix with ginger, coconut aminos, red bell pepper, and a ½ tsp each of salt and black pepper.
3. Combine green onions, chili pepper, and cilantro in a bowl, drizzle with orange juice, add salt and black pepper to taste and toss.
4. Stack two leaves Boston lettuce on flat surface, spoon in some of the Tilapia filling, top with orange cilantro salad, wrap, and enjoy.

Note: You can also wrap your fish tacos in flaxseed tortillas (recipe in Sides and Accompaniments).

Nutrition (per serving)
Calories 228 g
Carbs 5 g
Fat 11 g
Protein 30 g
Sodium 474 mg
Sugar 3 g

Garlic Shrimp in Mushroom Vestibules

Serve: 4
Preparation time: 15 minutes
Cooking time: 35 minutes

Ingredients:

½ lb shrimp
½ red bell pepper, seeded, finely-chopped
1 celery stalk, finely chopped
4 Portabella mushrooms
1 cup coconut milk
¼ cup ghee, melted
1 lemon, juiced
½ tsp rosemary
1 tsp salt
1 tsp black pepper
Extra virgin olive oil

Directions:

1. Preheat oven to 400ºF.
2. Heat ghee in cast iron skillet, add garlic, bell pepper, and celery stalk, and sauté for two minutes.
3. Add shrimp, salt, black pepper, and rosemary, and sauté until shrimp is pink. Remove shrimp and veggies to plate.
4. In the same skillet, place portabella mushrooms upside down in skillet.
5. Spoon equal amount shrimp in each Portabella mushrooms, pour coconut milk over each Portabella mushroom, allowing it to leak into skillet.
6. Place into oven, and bake for 25 minutes.

Nutrition per serving (g)

Calories 385 g

Fat 35 g

Carbs 6 g

Protein 15 g

Sodium 733 mg

Sugar 3 g

Serves: 6
Preparation time: 10 minutes
Cooking time: 25 minutes

Ingredients:
1 lb Andouille sausages
1 lb shrimp
1 red bell pepper, seeded, diced
1 green bell pepper, seeded, diced
1 carrot, peeled, diced
1 celery stalk, diced
1 red onion, sliced
1 cup cauliflower florets, grated
2 cups tomatoes, diced
2 cups low-sodium chicken stock
1 tsp black pepper
1 tsp salt
1 bay leaf
Extra virgin olive oil

Directions:
1. Slice Andouille sausage into ½" thick slices.
2. Heat 3 tbsp. extra virgin olive oil in cast iron skillet over medium heat.
3. Add onion and garlic, and sauté.
4. Add bell peppers, celery stalk, and carrot, and sauté for 3 minutes.
5. Add tomatoes, chicken stock, black pepper, salt, bay leaf, and cauliflower.
6. Cover skillet, and cook for 20 minutes over medium heat.
7. Add shrimp, cook for a minute, and remove from heat.

8. Serve hot.

Nutrition per serving:
Calories 648 g
Carbs 20 g
Fat 40 g
Sodium 2324 mg
Protein 50 g
Sugar 8 g

VEGETARIAN

Hot and Crispy Vegetable Salad

Serves: 4
Preparation time: 15 minutes
Cooking time: 15 minutes

Ingredients:
1 small head cauliflower
4 asparagus spears
2 cups Brussels sprouts
½ cup walnuts
3 eggs, boiled
½ cup water.
1 lemon, juiced
1 tsp salt
1 tsp black pepper
Extra virgin olive oil

Directions:
1. Separate cauliflower into florets.
2. Slice asparagus into 1" pieces.
3. Heat 4 tbsp. extra virgin olive oil into cast iron skillet over medium heat.
4. Add asparagus, cauliflower, Brussels sprouts, sauté.
5. Add water, cover, and allow to steam for 10 minutes.
6. Add lemon juice, salt, and black pepper.
7. Slice boiled eggs into 4 wedges.
8. Top salad with boiled eggs, walnuts, and serve.

Nutrition (per serving)

Calories 241 g

Carbs 10 g

Fat 20 g

Protein 11 g

Sodium 78 mg

Sugar 3 g

Cauliflower and Sweet Potato Curry

Serves: 4
Preparation time: 10 minutes
Cooking time: 35 minutes

Ingredients:
1 medium head cauliflower
1 sweet potato
1 carrot, died
1 medium onion, diced
1 medium tomato, diced
4 cloves garlic, minced
1 tbsp chopped ginger
1 tbsp organic tomato paste
½ tsp cumin seed
½ tsp turmeric
1 tsp paprika
1 tsp black pepper
1 tsp salt
¼ cup ghee

Directions:
1. Peel sweet potato, and slice into 1" pieces.
2. Chop cauliflower into small florets, remove tough skin from cauliflower stem and chop into ½" pieces.
3. Heat ghee, add cumin seeds, toast for 30 seconds.
4. Add onion and garlic, and sauté for a minute, add tomato, ginger, turmeric, and paprika, and cook for 3 minutes.
5. Mix in tomato paste, add sweet potato, carrot, cauliflower, black pepper, salt.

6. Reduce heat to medium low, cover and cook for 30 minutes, or until cauliflower and sweet potato are tender.
7. Serve with Flaxseed tortilla (recipe in Sides and Accompaniments).

Nutrition (per serving)
Calories 214 g
Carbs 22 g
Fat 13 g
Protein 5 g
Sodium 654 mg
Sugar 9 g

Garlic Asparagus Sauté

Serves: 4
Preparation time: 10 min.
Cooking time: 30 minutes

Ingredients:
1 lb asparagus spears
1 red onion, sliced
2 cloves garlic
½ cup cashews, crushed
1 onion, juiced
1 tsp salt, black pepper
Extra virgin olive oil

Directions:
1. Heat 4 tbsp. extra virgin olive oil in skillet.
2. Add onion and garlic, and sauté for a minute.
3. Add asparagus spears, cashew, salt, black pepper, and vegetable stock. Cover and cook on low for 25 minutes or until asparagus is tender.
4. Uncover and allow liquid to evaporate if still remaining.
5. Drizzle with lemon juice before serving.

Nutrition (per serving)
Calories 205 g
Carbs 16 g
Fat 15 g
Sodium 589 mg
Protein 6 g
Sugar 5 g

Veggie Lasagna

Serves: 8
Prep Time: 15 minutes.
Cooking time: 50 minutes

Ingredients:

4 Chinese eggplants
1 green bell pepper, seeded, sliced
1 medium onion, diced
4 cloves garlic
¼ cup Macadamia nuts, chopped
¼ cup cashews, chopped
2 cups pureed tomato
1 lemon, juiced
½ tsp black pepper
1 tsp salt
Extra virgin olive oil

Directions:

1. Slice eggplant in half horizontally and in half again vertically, scoop out approximately 1tbsp eggplant flesh from each eggplant.
2. Heat 4 tbsp. extra virgin olive oil in cast iron skillet.
3. Add garlic, onion, and bell pepper. Sauté.
4. Add scooped eggplant flesh, sauté for another minute.
5. Pour tomato puree into skillet, mix.
6. Set eggplant in skillet flesh-side up.
7. Spoon tomato puree mixture on top of eggplant, sprinkle with nuts.
8. Cover skillet, and bake in oven for 40 minutes.

Nutrition (per serving)

Calories 485 g

Carbs 55 g

Fat 28 g

Protein 11 g

Sodium 46 mg

Sugar 26 g

Creamy Zucchini Slides

Serves: 8
Preparation time: 5 minutes.
Cooking time: 40 minutes

Ingredients:
4 zucchinis, stemmed
1 red bell pepper, diced
4 cloves garlic, minced
1 can coconut milk
¼ tsp horseradish
½ tsp paprika
Coconut oil

Directions:
1. Slice zucchini in half.
2. Heat 4 tbsp. coconut oil in cast iron skillet.
3. Add garlic, bell pepper, and horseradish. Sauté.
4. Add zucchini, flesh side down, and brown for a minute, turn over.
5. Pour in coconut milk, sprinkle paprika, salt, and black pepper.
6. Cover skillet, and cook on low for 30 minutes.

Nutrition (per serving)
Calories 243 g
Carbs 13 g
Fat 22 g
Protein 4 g
Sodium 31 mg
Sugar 7 g

SIDES AND ACCOMPANIMENTS

ZuCa Noodles

Serves: 4
Preparation time: 10 minutes
Cooking time: 0 minutes

Ingredients
3 zucchini
1 carrot
½ tsp salt
Extra virgin olive oil

Directions:
1. Peel zucchini and carrot.
2. Use a vegetable peeler, and peel zucchini until you reach seedy center. Save center for another recipe.
3. With the same vegetable peeler, peel carrot wisps.
4. Combine zucchini and carrots with 3 tbsp. extra light olive oil, ½ tsp salt.

Nutrition (per serving)
Calories 120 g
Carbs 6 g
Fat 11 g
Protein 2 g
Sodium 316 mg
Sugar 3 g

Cauliflower Flecked with Basil and Pine Nut

Serves: 4
Preparation time: 10 minutes
Cooking time: 10 minutes

Ingredients:
½ medium cauliflower
½ cup medium purple cauliflower
¼ cup pine nuts
¼ cup basil
½ lemon, juiced
1 tsp black pepper
1 tsp salt
Extra virgin olive oil

Directions:
1. Slice cauliflower into small florets and salt.
2. Heat extra virgin olive oil, add cauliflower, and sauté for 5 minutes.
3. Add pine nuts, black pepper, continue to sauté for another minute.
4. Remove from heat, drizzle with lemon juice, sprinkle with basil, mix, and serve.

Nutrition (per serving)
Calories 245 g
Carbs 10 g
Fat 24 g
Protein 4 g
Sodium 620 mg
Sugar 4 g

Serves: 6
Preparation time: 15 minutes
Cooking time: 5 minutes

Ingredients:
1¼ cup flax meal
1 tbsp tapioca flour
¼ cup almond milk, warm
¼ tsp salt
Extra virgin olive oil

Directions:
1. Combine flax meal, tapioca flour, and salt, and knead with almond milk.
2. Divide dough into six balls.
3. Place a piece of parchment paper on a flat surface, drop your ball of dough on parchment, and place a second piece of parchment on top.
4. Using rolling pin, roll your flaxseed tortilla.
5. Heat 3 tbsp. olive oil in cast iron skillet.
6. Place flaxseed tortilla in skillet, cook for 1-1/2 minute per side.

Nutrition (per serving)
Calories 331
Carbs 23 g
Fat 27 g
Protein 8 g
Sodium 100 mg
Sugar 0 g

Paleo Ranch Dressing

Serves: 8
Prep Time: 5 minutes.
Cooking time: 0 minutes

Ingredients:
1 egg
½ cup coconut milk
½ lemon, juiced
½ tsp dry mustard
1 tsp dill
½ tsp ground black pepper
½ tsp salt
¾ cup almond oil

Directions:
1. Remove egg from refrigerator an hour before preparation.
2. Place egg in blender and mix, add remaining ingredients, and blend until smooth.

Nutrition (per serving)
Calories 225
Carbs 1 g
Fat 25 g
Protein 1 g
Sodium 158 mg
Sugar 1 g

Toasted Pecan and Cranberry Salad

Serve: 4
Preparation time: 5 minutes
Cooking time: 2 minutes

Ingredients:

¼ cup pecans
¼ cup walnuts
2 tbsp sunflower seeds
½ cup cashew
¼ cup dried cranberries
1 medium cucumber
1 cup arugula
1 cup red leaf lettuce
3 lemons, juiced
1 tsp black pepper
1 tsp salt
Extra virgin olive oil

Directions:

1. Chop cashews and mix with juice of 2 lemons, let sit overnight.
2. Heat 3 tbsp. extra light olive in cast iron skillet.
3. Add pecans, walnuts, and sunflower seeds, and toast for two minutes, continually stirring.
4. Remove nuts from skillet.
5. Slice cucumber into ½" thick slices.
6. Combine cucumber with cranberries, arugula, and red leaf lettuce.
7. In a bowl, combine juice of one lemon and ¼ cup extra light olive oil, salt and black pepper.
8. Toss salad with lemon dressing, toss with toasted nuts and seeds just before serving.

Nutrition (per serving)

Calories 321 g

Fat 29 g

Carbs 16 g

Protein 7 g

Sodium 595 mg

Sugar 0 g

CONCLUSION

Switching to a Paleo lifestyle is a big decision, but once you do it, you are going to be in it for the long haul because the health benefits are quickly evident. Most converts to Paleo enjoy the benefits, but they often have difficulty in designing quick, delicious meals for those days when spending a few hours in the kitchen is just not an option.

Thanks to cast iron cookware, Paleo cooking is made a whole lot easier. Brightly-colored vegetables, heart-healthy nuts, and beautiful cuts of poultry, meat, and fish are combined to create heart-healthy, brain-boosting dishes that will keep you and your family deliciously-fuelled. The Delicious Paleo Cast Iron Recipes cookbook will surely make life a much simpler with tasty Paleo treats every night of the week!

ABOUT THE AUTHOR

Louise Davidson is an avid cook who likes simple flavors and easy-to-make meals. She lives in Tennessee with her husband, her three grown children, her two dogs, and the family's cat Whiskers. She loves the outdoor and has mastered the art of camp cooking on open fires and barbecue grills.

In colder months, she loves to whip up some slow cooker meals, and uses her favorite cooking tools in her kitchen, the cast iron pans, and Dutch oven. She also is very busy preparing Christmas treats for her extended family and friends. She gets busy baking for the holiday season sometimes as early as October. Her recipes are cherished by everyone who has tasted her foods and holiday treats.

Louise is a part-time writer of cookbooks, sharing her love of food, her experience, and her family's secret recipes with her readers.

She also loves to learn and share tips and tricks to make life easier.

Other books from Louise include:

Please click on the book cover if you would like to check it out.

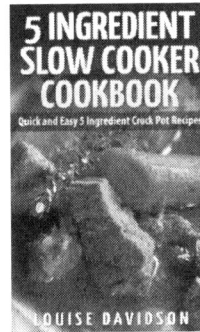

APPENDIX

Cooking Conversion Charts

1. Volumes

US Fluid Oz.	US	US Dry Oz.	Metric Liquid ml
¼ oz.	2 tsp.	1 oz.	10 ml.
½ oz.	1 tbsp.	2 oz.	15 ml.
1 oz.	2 tbsp.	3 oz.	30 ml.
2 oz.	¼ cup	3½ oz.	60 ml.
4 oz.	½ cup	4 oz.	125 ml.
6 oz.	¾ cup	6 oz.	175 ml.
8 oz.	1 cup	8 oz.	250 ml.

Tsp.= teaspoon - tbsp.= tablespoon – oz.= ounce – ml.= millimeter

2. Oven Temperatures

Celsius (ºC)	Fahrenheit (ºF)
90	220
110	225
120	250
140	275
150	300
160	325
180	350
190	375
200	400
215	425
230	450
250	475
260	500

PALEO RESSOURCES

Here are a few suggestions for those needing information on the Paleo diet.

A few books to read that I would recommend include:

The Paleo Diet Revised by Dr. Loren Cardain
Paleo Diet for Beginners by Madison Miller
Nom Nom Paleo: Food for Humans by Michelle Tam and Heny Fong

Interesting websites for Paleo diet followers:

http://robbwolf.com/what-is-the-paleo-diet/
http://thepaleodiet.com/
http://ultimatepaleoguide.com/
http://nomnompaleo.com/paleo101

42766964R00052

Made in the USA
Lexington, KY
04 July 2015